Pluto and the
for New P

By Gregory Vogt

STECK-VAUGHN
ELEMENTARY · SECONDARY · ADULT · LIBRARY

A Harcourt Company

www.steck-vaughn.com

Photo Acknowledgments
Dr. R. Albrecht, ESA/ESO Space Telescope European Coordinating Facility and NASA, title page; NASA, cover, 6, 14, 16, 20, 22, 24, 28, 30, 32, 39; Solar & Heliospheric Observatory (SOHO), 10. SOHO is a project of international cooperation between ESA and NASA. Erich Karkoschka (University of Arizona) and NASA, 12; Bettmann/CORBIS, 18; A. Stern (SwRI), M. Buie (Lowell Obs.), NASA, ESA, 26; C. Grady (NOAO at NASA Goddard Space Flight Center) and NASA, 40; Hubble Heritage Team (AURA/STScI/ NASA), 44

Contents

Diagram of Pluto

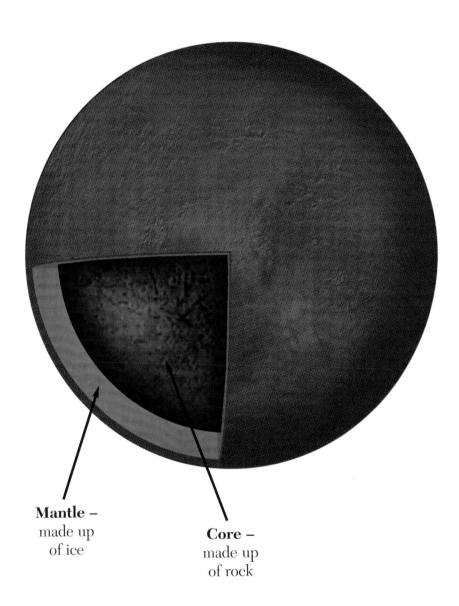

Mantle –
made up
of ice

Core –
made up
of rock

What is Pluto?

Pluto is the ninth planet in our solar system. It is the farthest planet from the Sun.

What is Pluto made of?

Pluto is the only planet that is made mainly of rock and ice.

How big is Pluto?

Pluto is the smallest known planet in our solar system. It is only 1,430 miles (2,301 km) in diameter. Diameter is the distance through the center of a circle.

Does Pluto have a moon?

Pluto has one moon that orbits it. The moon's name is Charon. Charon is half the size of Pluto.

What is Pluto like?

Pluto is dark and cold. It is too far away from the Sun to receive much light or heat.

This white streak of stars is called the Milky Way.

Early Astronomy

In ancient times, people did not understand the objects in the night sky. Every night, thousands of stars seemed to move across the sky. People did not know that stars are balls of very hot gases that give off heat and light. They did not know that Earth spins. Today, people know that the stars do not travel across the sky. It is Earth's spin that makes the stars seem to move.

Astronomers are scientists who study objects in space. Early astronomers carefully studied stars in the sky. They watched five special objects in the night sky. These objects stood out because they were in different places in the sky each night. They did not follow the same path as the rest of the objects in the sky.

Names

Early astronomers named each of the five oddly moving objects after gods and goddesses in Roman myths. A myth is a story told to explain things in nature.

One object they named Mercury. Mercury was the messenger. Another object they named Venus. Venus was the goddess of love and beauty in Roman myths. The three other objects they named Mars, Jupiter, and Saturn. In the Roman myths, Mars is the Roman god of war. Jupiter is the ruler of the gods. And Saturn is the god of agriculture.

Planets in our Solar System

Today, astronomers know that the five objects are planets. Planets are ball-shaped worlds that travel around a star. Planets do not give off light. They reflect light from the star they orbit.

The Sun is a star. The planets travel around the Sun in paths called orbits. There are nine planets that orbit the Sun. The Sun and all the objects that orbit around it make up our solar system.

The planet closest to the Sun is Mercury. The next closest planet is Venus. Farther away is Earth, then Mars, Jupiter, Saturn, Uranus, Neptune, and Pluto.

This diagram shows the location of planets in our solar system. The sizes and distances are not to scale.

Sun

Mercury

Venus

Earth

Mars

Jupiter

Saturn

Uranus

Neptune

Pluto

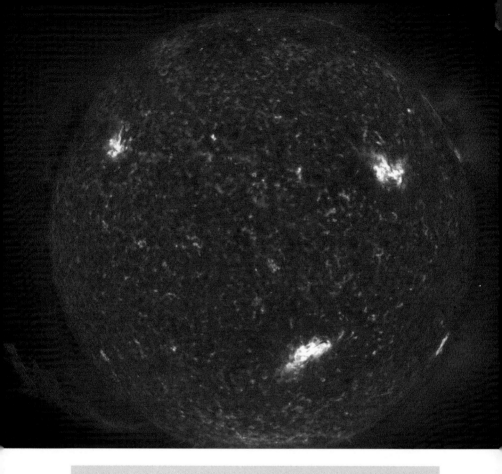

> The Sun's high density gives it the greatest gravitational pull in the solar system.

Gravity and the Sun

The Sun is the solar system's largest and densest object. Density is the amount of matter squeezed into a certain space. Matter is anything that has weight and takes up space. Tightly packed matter in a small area is said to be massive or to have a high density. The denser an object is, the more it pulls on objects around it. This pull is an object's gravity. Gravity is a natural force that attracts objects to each other.

The Sun has a stronger gravitational pull than any other object in our solar system. The closer a planet is to the Sun, the more the Sun's gravitational force affects it.

Early Beliefs

Early astronomers believed the night sky was a great black shell surrounding Earth. They thought that the stars were lights on the shell. They also thought that the Sun and the Moon were on the shell.

These early astronomers believed the shell spun around Earth. They thought that the stars moved because the shell was spinning. Astronomers thought planets were on their own shells because the planets did not move in the same way as the stars.

Until the 1700s, astronomers knew of only five planets besides Earth. These were the close planets Mercury, Venus, Mars, Jupiter, and Saturn. They were very bright and easy to see. Astronomers did not know about the three planets farthest away from Earth. These planets are too dim to be seen with just the eye.

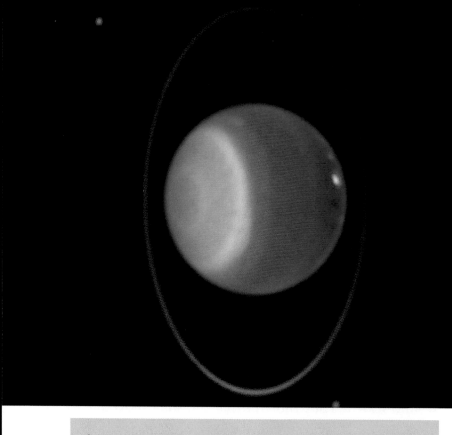

 William Herschel discovered Uranus (YOOR-uh-nuhs).

Discovery of Uranus

Astronomers needed a new tool to see dim, faraway objects. They needed a tool that made distant objects appear bigger and brighter. The tool they invented was the telescope.

Scientists Hans Lippershey and Galileo Galilei made the first telescopes in 1608 and 1609. Galileo made many discoveries about stars with his telescope. He studied a white streak in the night sky called the Milky Way. He learned that the white streak was the combined light of many stars.

Sir William Herschel also made telescopes. In 1781, he was looking through one of the telescopes he had built. He aimed the telescope at a group of stars.

Among the stars, Herschel spotted a blue-green dot. He watched the path of the dot over several nights. He realized that it moved like a planet and not like a star. Herschel's blue dot was another planet.

Herschel named the new planet Georgium Sidus, which means Star of George. The name was in honor of his patron, Great Britain's King George III. A patron is somebody who gives money so a person can work on special projects.

The name of Herschel's planet changed twice. For a time, it was called Herschel in honor of its discoverer. In the early 1800s, the name Uranus was suggested by astronomer Johann Elert Bode. In Greek myths, Uranus is the god of the heavens. By the late 1800s, Herschel's planet became known to everyone as Uranus.

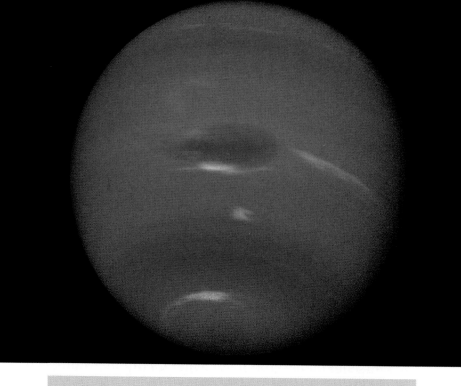

Telescopes and Planet Hunting

Astronomers now knew of seven planets in the solar system. Some wondered if there might be more planets beyond Uranus. The telescopes the astronomers used were not strong enough to see any other planets. Planet hunting with telescopes can be difficult. Only nearby planets can be seen easily.

Telescopes use lenses and mirrors to collect light. To collect light from faraway objects, lenses and mirrors must be large. The larger the lenses and mirrors are, the more light they collect.

In fact, telescopes collect too much light for astronomers to see planets outside the solar system. The brightness of faraway stars covers up any planets that might circle them. Astronomers cannot see these planets with a telescope. To make their next discoveries, astronomers turned to mathematics.

Discovering Neptune

In early 1846, astronomers watched Uranus moving oddly in its orbit. They had been studying Uranus and had mapped what they thought was its normal movement. But sometimes Uranus was moving faster or slower than astronomers expected.

Some astronomers thought a planet was changing Uranus's orbit. They thought this new planet's gravity was the force making Uranus go faster and slower.

Using mathematics, astronomer Urbain Jean Joseph Leverrier predicted where the new planet would be. Later in 1846, Johann Gottfried Galle aimed a telescope at Leverrier's predicted location. He found the eighth planet. The new planet was named Neptune. Neptune is farther away and fainter than Uranus. It is nearly 2.9 billion miles (4.7 billion km) from the Sun.

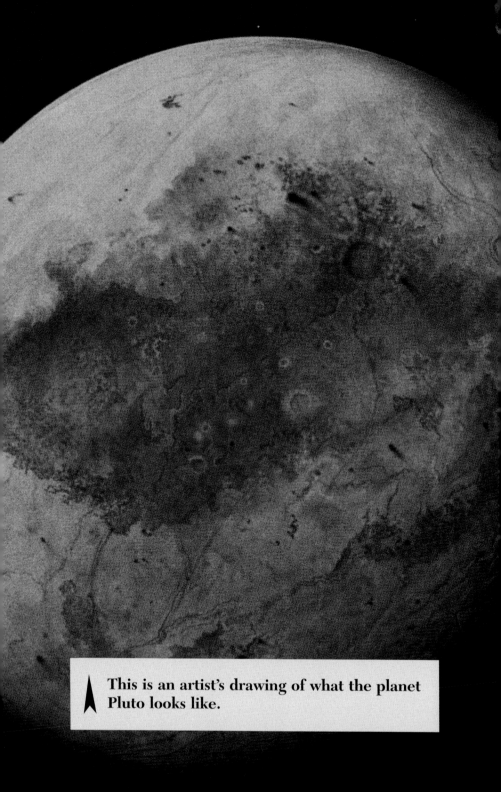

This is an artist's drawing of what the planet Pluto looks like.

Pluto, the Ninth Planet

Neptune's motions puzzled astronomers. They decided that there must be another planet orbiting the Sun. They felt that this planet's gravitational force was pulling on Neptune and causing it to move oddly. Some astronomers nicknamed the mystery planet "Planet X."

In the early 1900s, Percival Lowell was one of the astronomers who believed that there was a Planet X. Lowell had an observatory in Flagstaff, Arizona. An observatory is a building with a large telescope inside it. Lowell's observatory sat on a high hill where the night sky was very dark. It was the perfect place to use a telescope.

Lowell searched for Planet X for 11 years. He died before the planet was discovered.

Search for Planet X

In 1905, Lowell decided to look for Planet X. Lowell searched for Planet X secretly. He did not want other astronomers to know what he was doing. If they did, Lowell was afraid they might make the discovery first.

Lowell began taking photographs of the night sky. A few days later, he took another photograph of the same section of sky. Lowell looked at the photographs with a magnifying glass. He looked for any star that seemed to move. If he found such a star, he knew it would not be a star at all. It would be Planet X.

Lowell worked hard and his health suffered. In 1912, he collapsed. He later recovered, but he knew he needed to find a better way to look for Planet X.

The new tool Lowell found was called a blink comparator. The blink comparator projected pictures on a screen. The pictures flashed back and forth. First, Lowell would see one picture of the sky. Then he would see the second picture of the sky. This made it easier to see if an object had moved.

But even with the blink comparator, Lowell never found Planet X. He died in 1916, 14 years before Planet X was discovered.

This is a photograph of the pictures Tombaugh used to discover Pluto.

Clyde Tombaugh

Clyde Tombaugh grew up on a farm. He loved astronomy and built his own telescopes using parts from machines on his father's farm. He looked at Mars and Jupiter and sketched what he saw.

In 1928, Tombaugh sent his sketches to the Lowell Observatory. Astronomers at the observatory liked Tombaugh's pictures. They asked Tombaugh to come to the observatory to work. Tombaugh arrived there in 1929.

At the Lowell Observatory, Tombaugh's only job was to search for Planet X. For months, he used a telescope to take pictures of the night sky. After waiting several days, he took more pictures of the same places.

Like Lowell, Tombaugh used a blink comparator to look at both pictures. Tombaugh looked for objects that moved. That meant that they had changed position between the time the two pictures were taken.

Not many visiting astronomers took Tombaugh's search seriously. They laughed at Tombaugh when they visited the Lowell Observatory. They did not think that he would find anything with his improved blink comparator. They did not think it was possible to find another planet. They thought the planet would be too far away to see.

But on February 18, 1930, Tombaugh proved them wrong. He compared two pictures with the blink comparator. He noticed that a tiny dot had moved. The tiny dot looked just like any other star. Tombaugh saw millions of dim stars just like it. But stars do not move. Tombaugh had found Planet X.

Naming Planet X

Naming the new planet was almost as hard as
finding it. Many different people and newspapers
suggested names for Planet X. Lowell's wife first
wanted the new planet to be named after her
husband. Then she wanted it to be named
Constance, after herself. One astronomer at the
observatory wanted to name the new planet Minerva.
In Roman myths, Minerva is the goddess of wisdom.

An 11-year-old schoolgirl named Venetia Burney
suggested the name Pluto for the planet. In Roman

myths, Pluto was god of the underworld. The underworld is where people went after they died. People felt that the name suited the planet. Pluto is so far away that it is dark and cold like the underworld. Also, the first two letters of Pluto are P and L. These were Percival Lowell's initials. Pluto turned out to be the perfect name.

Studying Pluto

After Tombaugh's discovery, astronomers began studying Pluto. But Pluto is very hard to see and study. It is tiny and far away. Not much sunlight reaches Pluto. Even less reflects back. Even the most powerful telescopes cannot make Pluto clear enough for astronomers to see it well.

Pluto is the smallest known planet in the solar system. It is only 1,430 miles (2,301 km) in diameter. Diameter is the distance through the center of a circle. Earth is more than five times larger than Pluto. Earth's diameter is about 7,926 miles (12,756 km). Pluto would fit inside the borders of the United States.

Pluto's Orbit

It takes Pluto a long time to orbit the Sun. It orbits at an average distance of about 3.7 billion miles (5.9 billion km) from the Sun. Pluto takes 248 Earth years to travel around the Sun. Because it is so far away from the Sun, Pluto is a cold planet. Its average temperature is –431° Fahrenheit (–222° C).

Astronomers have studied Pluto's orbit. They have learned that its orbit is unlike the orbits of the other planets in our solar system. The orbits of the other eight planets are almost perfect circles. But Pluto's orbit is elliptical. Elliptical means shaped like a stretched-out circle.

Until they studied Pluto's orbit, astronomers had thought that the solar system was nearly flat. But Pluto's orbit is not the same as the other planets' orbits. Pluto's orbit is tilted about 17° from the other planets' orbits.

Because of its elliptical orbit, Pluto is not always the same distance away from the Sun. During one part of its orbit, it is about 4.6 billion miles (7.4 billion km) from the Sun. During another part of its orbit, it is only about 2.7 billion miles (4.3 billion km) from the Sun.

Along part of Pluto's orbit, it is closer to the Sun than Neptune is. During that time, Neptune is the most distant planet from the Sun. This part of Pluto's orbit lasts 20 years. It last happened from February 1979 to February 1999. It will not happen again until the year 2228.

Pluto's Surface

Astronomers have many questions about Pluto. They want to know what its surface is like. They want to know if it has an atmosphere. An atmosphere is a layer of gases that surrounds an object in space. No space probe has ever flown near Pluto. A space probe is a craft built to explore and gather information about space.

The Hubble Space Telescope took the best pictures of Pluto. The Hubble is a powerful telescope on a spacecraft that orbits Earth. The Hubble's pictures show light and dark patches on Pluto's surface. From these pictures, astronomers can see that Pluto looks something like Neptune's moon Triton.

Triton is the largest of Neptune's moons. It can be seen from Earth. In 1989, astronomers learned a lot about Triton when the *Voyager 2* space probe flew by and took pictures of it. Astronomers saw that the surface of Triton is made from rock and ice.

Astronomers think that Pluto is also made of rock, ice, and frozen gases. Craters and other features on its surface may cause Pluto's patches. They may also be caused by frost that moves across Pluto's surface as the seasons change. Astronomers do not know for sure what causes the light and dark patches.

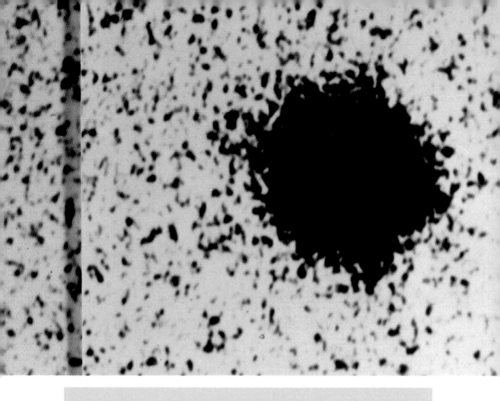

> ▲ **This is the picture that Christy used to discover Charon. The moon is the black spot.**

Charon

For many years, astronomers thought Pluto had no moons. But in 1978, astronomer James Christy was looking at pictures of Pluto. The pictures were not very clear. But Christy noticed something strange. Pluto seemed to have a bump on it.

Christy looked at other pictures of Pluto. He saw the bump again. But the bump was in different places. Christy realized that it was not a bump at all. It was a moon orbiting Pluto.

system with an atmosphere. Astronomers think that this atmosphere is really Pluto's. They think that Charon is so close to Pluto that Charon orbits within Pluto's atmosphere.

Astronomers have learned the most about Charon from pictures taken by the Hubble. The pictures show that Charon's color is different than Pluto's color. Astronomers study the different colors to figure out what materials the planet and moon are made from. They think Pluto's surface is rock and solid methane, and its atmosphere is rich in methane gas. They think that the surface of Charon is ice.

The Minor Planet

Some astronomers believe that Pluto is not a planet for several reasons. First, it is the only planet made of rock and frozen gases. Second, it is so much smaller than the other planets. Third, its orbit is different from all the other planets.

Some astronomers think that Pluto is really an asteroid. An asteroid is a large, irregularly shaped rock in space. Most asteroids are only a few miles in diameter. The largest known asteroid is Ceres. It is almost 600 miles (966 km) in diameter. Most asteroids in the solar system orbit the Sun in the asteroid belt. This area between Mars and Jupiter is full of thousands of asteroids.

Astronomers who say Pluto is a planet point out that asteroids are irregularly shaped. But Pluto is round, like a planet. They also point out that asteroids are not large enough to have atmospheres. But Pluto has an atmosphere, like a planet.

Other astronomers think Pluto is really a comet. A comet is a large ball of ice, dust, and rock. Many comets travel in orbits that bring them close to the Sun. The Sun's heat melts some of the ice. Gases stream off and form a tail. Some astronomers think Pluto's frozen surface might form a tail if it passed near the sun. Astronomers who say Pluto is a planet point out that Pluto is much larger than any comet.

Still other astronomers say that Pluto is a different kind of planet. They say that it is a minor planet, and the rest of the planets are major planets. Calling it a minor planet has settled the argument for many astronomers.

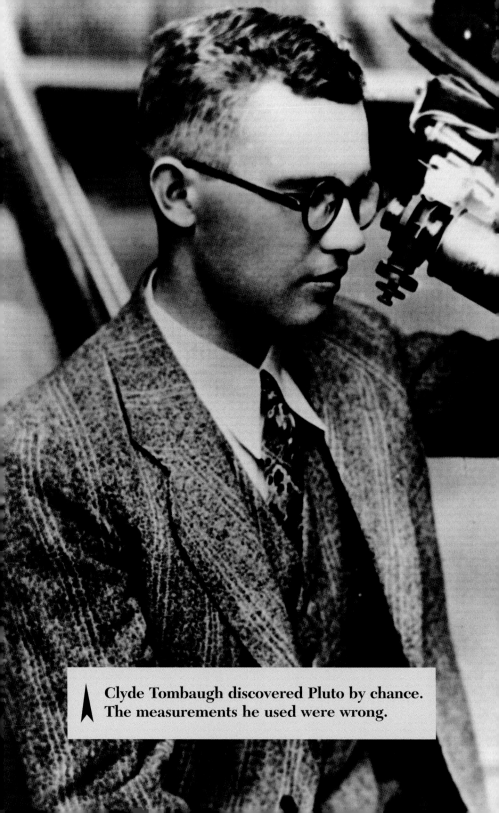

Clyde Tombaugh discovered Pluto by chance.
The measurements he used were wrong.

Planet Hunting

When Tombaugh looked for Pluto, he used Percival Lowell's measurements of Neptune's orbit to aim his telescope. Other astronomers checked these measurements. They also looked closely at Pluto's gravitational pull. They found that Neptune is more than 8,000 times more massive than Pluto. That means Pluto is much too small to have an effect on Neptune. Astronomers found that the measurements Tombaugh used were wrong. He had discovered Pluto by chance.

Astronomers had a new problem. Something unknown was causing the changes in Neptune's orbit. Astronomers began looking for another Planet X.

If there is another Planet X, Astronomers think it is beyond Pluto. It might be the same size as Pluto. If so, it would be very difficult to find.

Planet Hunting with Space Probes

Scientists want to get closer to planets than they can with telescopes. They want to study the planets close up. That is why they send space probes out into the solar system. The space probes send back information that helps the scientists learn.

Scientists use a planet's gravity to help steer the space probes. When a probe comes close to a planet, the planet's gravity pulls on it. This speeds up the probe. It also pulls the probe into a path that curves around the planet. Scientists use this curving to change a space probe's path. That way, the space probe can visit other planets.

In 1972 and 1973, scientists launched the *Pioneer 10* and *Pioneer 11* space probes. These probes passed through the asteroid belt and flew near Jupiter in December 1973 and December 1974. *Pioneer 10* then continued on its way out of the solar system. It was the first space probe sent beyond the solar system. *Pioneer 11* flew by Saturn in September 1979.

In 1977, scientists launched the *Voyager 1* and *Voyager 2* space probes. These probes flew near Jupiter in 1979. They passed the giant planet, taking pictures and measurements. Jupiter's gravity redirected the probes. They were sent into space.

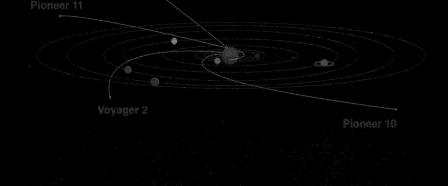

> **This diagram shows the paths the different space probes traveled.**

Each of the *Pioneer* and *Voyager* probes is headed in a different direction.

Scientists are tracking the journeys of these space probes. They are hoping that one will pass near an unknown planet. Then the planet's gravity will change the space probe's path. This will help scientists know where to look for a new planet. But no space probe paths have been changed so far.

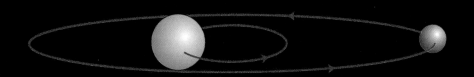

Pluto and Charon orbit each other.
This makes Pluto appear to wobble.

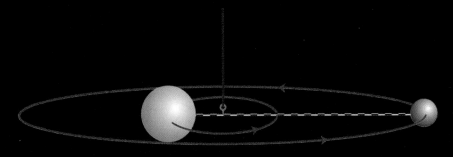

To see how this works, imagine two balls
connected by a stick. The balls are Pluto
and Charon. The stick represents gravity. The rope
is where Pluto and Charon are balanced.
When Pluto and Charon orbit, they twirl
around the balance point.

 This diagram of Pluto and Charon shows how wobbling happens.

Wobbling

It is possible that scientists have discovered all the planets orbiting the Sun. There might not be another Planet X. But astronomers are also looking for planets orbiting other stars.

To discover faraway planets, astronomers use telescopes in a special way. They do not use them to look directly at planets. Instead, they look for star wobble. Star wobble occurs when a star moves one way and then the other. Star wobble is movement caused by a planet's gravity. If the wobble repeats, astronomers know that there is a planet orbiting the star.

Astronomers can learn many things by watching stars wobble. If a star wobbles a long way back and forth, the planet orbiting the star is very massive. If a star wobbles only a little back and forth, the planet orbiting the star is not very massive. If a star wobbles back and forth quickly, the planet is in a close orbit around the star. If a star wobbles back and forth slowly, the planet is in a faraway orbit around the star.

Red Shift

In 1995, astronomers began to discover new planets. They used the wobble method to find some of them. The first ones they found were very large. These produced big wobbles in their stars. They were the easiest to see.

Astronomers have found other planets by watching to see if a star's color seems to change. If a star's color seems to change as astronomers watch it from Earth, it might mean that a planet is orbiting the star.

Stars that are tugged by a planet's gravitational force seem to change color only slightly. The stars look slightly redder if a planet's gravity pulls them away from Earth. They look slightly bluer if a planet's gravity pulls them toward Earth. This change in the appearance of the stars' color is known to astronomers as red shift.

Since 1995, astronomers have found more than 30 stars that have planets orbiting them. All of the new planets are very large. Because they are so large, astronomers compare the new planets to the size of Jupiter. Jupiter is the largest planet in our solar system. It is more than 1,300 times larger than Earth. Some of the newly discovered planets astronomers have found are only about half as large as Jupiter. Others are 11 times larger.

▲ Astronomers compare planets that orbit other stars to Jupiter.

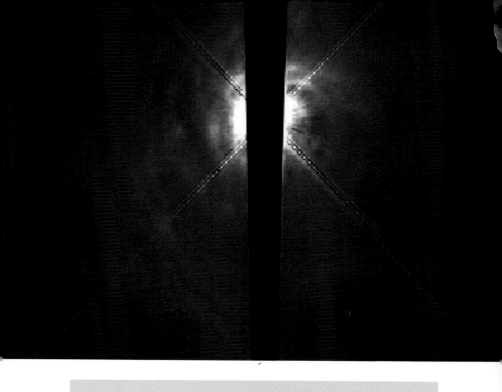

Scientists study stars like this to find planets. They use the black area to block starlight so they can study it. This star has a disk of gas and dust around it. Planets might form there.

Upsilon Andromedae

Astronomers have become better at finding new planets. With practice, they have begun to find smaller planets. Today, faraway planets the size of Saturn and Uranus have been found.

Astronomers have found one star that has at least three large planets orbiting it. The star is called Upsilon Andromedae. Upsilon Andromedae is a sunlike star. It is about three times as bright as the Sun and can be seen by the naked eye. It is about 44 light-years away from Earth. A light-year is the distance light travels in one Earth year. Astronomers use light-years when measuring great distances.

Astronomers believe that Upsilon Andromedae's planet system is a lot like our solar system. In 1996, astronomers found one planet very close to Upsilon Andromedae. The closet planet to the Sun in our solar system is Mercury. The planet closest to Upsilon Andromedae is much closer than Mercury is to our Sun. It is about 70% the mass of Jupiter.

The second and third planets orbiting Upsilon Andromedae were discovered in 1999. The second planet is about as far out as Earth is from the Sun. It is about twice the mass of Jupiter. The third planet orbiting Upsilon Andromedae is about three times farther away from the star than Earth is from the Sun. It is four times more massive than Jupiter.

Astronomers do not know if an Earth-sized planet is also orbiting Upsilon Andromedae. The gravity from such a planet would not be strong enough to change the movement or observed color of Upsilon Andromedae. Astronomers would not be able to see any changes in the star through their telescopes.

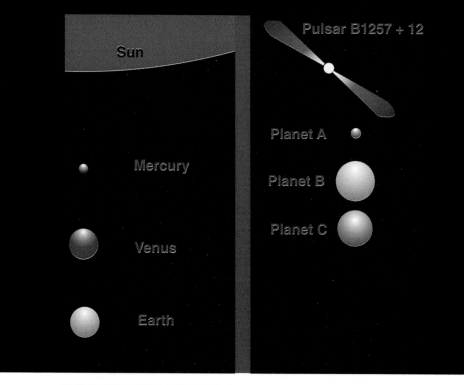

> **This diagram compares the planets around Pulsar B1257+12 to our inner solar system.**

Pulsar Planets

Astronomers study many different kinds of stars in the night sky. One special kind of star is called a pulsar. Pulsars are the smallest stars. They are usually only about 10 miles (16 km) across. All stars spin. But pulsars spin quickly because they are so small.

Each time a pulsar spins, it sends a wave of energy that travels to Earth. The pulses of energy travel through space like lighthouse signals. Each pulsar has its own pulse rate. It may pulse once every four seconds or hundreds of times per second. Each pulsar always pulses at the same rate.

Since 1967, astronomers have discovered hundreds of pulsars. In 1992, astronomer Alexander Wolszczan studied the pulsar called PSR B1257+12. He noticed that its pulse changed. He knew that a pulsar's pulse never changed. Something else had to be changing PSR B1257+12's pulse. Wolszczan discovered that three very small planets were orbiting PSR B1257+12. The gravity from the planets was changing the rate of PSR B1257+12's pulse.

Some astronomers think PSR B1257+12's planets were created from an explosion. They think an exploding star sent dust and gas into space. Gravity pulled the dust and gas together into clumps. Smaller clumps joined together when they crashed into each other. They became larger clumps. The clumps continued to grow over millions of years until they became the planets that now orbit PSR B1257+12.

Protoplanets

Our solar system is part of the Milky Way Galaxy. A galaxy is a very large system of stars and objects orbiting stars. A galaxy is held together by gravity. There are millions of stars in the Milky Way. With so many stars, there are many chances for planets to form around them. Astronomers will probably continue to find new planets in the Milky Way and in other galaxies.

Astronomers looking for new planets often study nebulas. Nebulas are large clouds of gas and dust. Sometimes astronomers see small objects forming in the nebulas. They think these objects are new planets. Astronomer call these new planets protoplanets.

Astronomers are always coming up with new tools to help them do their work. They build more powerful telescopes. They have also planned new space probes to find planets.

One new space probe is called the *Terrestrial Planet Finder*. Astronomers will use the *Terrestrial Planet Finder* to study planets and find new ones. Astronomers hope to launch the *Terrestrial Planet Finder* sometime around 2010.

Another planned space probe is called the *Kepler Mission*. *Kepler* will study the changes in brightness of about 900,000 stars. Some planets may pass in front of the star they are orbiting. If they do, the star will get dimmer because the planet blocks some of the star's light. The *Kepler Mission* would detect this. Scientists hope to find several hundred Earthlike planets. There is no launch date planned yet for the *Kepler Mission*.

Astronomers will use these new tools and invent others. They will continue to find more planets and make new discoveries.

Glossary

asteroid (AS-tuh-roid)—a giant space rock

astronomer (uh-STRON-uh-mer)—a scientist who studies objects in space

atmosphere (AT-muhss-fihr)—a layer of gases that surrounds a planet

comet (KOM-it)—a cluster of ice and rock that develops a tail of glowing gases as it nears the Sun

crater (KRAY-tur)—a bowl-shaped hole left when a meteorite strikes an object in space

galaxy (GAL-uhk-see)—a very large system of nebulas, stars, and orbiting objects that is held together by gravity

gravity (GRAV-uh-tee)—a force that attracts all objects to each other

nebula (NEB-yuh-luh)—a cloud of gas and dust in space

orbit (OR-bit)—the path an object travels around another object in space

planet (PLAN-it)—a large round object that orbits a star

protoplanet (PRO-tuh-plan-it)—a newly forming planet

pulsar (PUHL-sar)—a dense, rapidly spinning star that gives off waves of energy

Internet Sites and Addresses

Comets
http://www.windows.umich.edu/comets/comets.html

NASA for Kids
http://kids.msfc.nasa.gov

Planets and Moons
http://wwwflag.wr.usgs.gov/USGSFlag/Space/wall
/wall_txt.html

**Star Child: A Learning Center for
  Young Astronomers**
http://starchild.gsfc.nasa.gov/docs/StarChild/
  StarChild.html

NASA Headquarters
Washington, DC 20546-0001

The Planetary Society
65 North Catalina Avenue
Pasadena, CA 91106-2301

Index